Copyright © 2019 Diana Escalera
 All rights reserved. No parts of this publication may be reproduced, stored in retrieval system, or transmitted in any forms or by any means (including electronic, mechanical, photocopying, recording or otherwise) without prior written permission from the publisher.

Cover images Copyright © 2019 by Diana Escalera

ISBN: 978-0-359-38301-6

INTRODUCTION

This tells me that you're curious about this book. That you are ready to see with your own eyes, what "Eye Survived" really means. Our eyes have seen how life can make us or break us. Let me ask you this: What is Survival? According to Merriam Webster, "Survival, is the continuation of life or existence." To EXIST. To LIVE. So, what does that have to do with our eyes?

Try to remember of the times you have been through life challenges that has pushed you to your limits. A situation at your job, with your business, with a loved one, with a friend or even with yourself. Things and people that could have made you a "victim" in life. Victims are dead bodies. You are not a victim. You are a SURVIVOR.

SURVIVAL is what this book gives you. To be able to see yourself in my eyes as you read. To really look past my traumas and see how I used them to survive. To see that you too have survived your yesterdays! My life is just a piece of life that breaks into pieces of everyone's life. We are all connected because we are each other's story. This book is just not about my survival, but about yours. This book entails memories I recall from childhood to adolescent, but just not any memories. Memories that connected me to who I was growing up. Memories my subconscious mind try to once bury. These memories were delayed and will show itself at unusual timing. I call it: SURVIVAL MODE. Knowing what I know now, my body, mind and spirit was protecting me from becoming a victim. In this book, there are blank pages as well, to allow you to express yourself and to tell your OWN story.

Before you turn this page, I want you to do one thing. Have an open mind. Allow yourself to feel. Release your vulnerability onto these pages and BREATHE.

Now let's SURVIVE together!

What My Eyes Have Seen

I always knew I was different from other kids. I acted different, I walked different, I even thought differently. At 5yro, I realize how different I was. I always felt like I was here, before I was born. I also became intrigued with people's pain. I somehow always found beauty in it. Something most kids wouldn't have understood my age. I was curious about the

human mind. What I didn't know is that I will soon experience every pain that captivated my curiosity.

I remember wanting to escape my empty home at 5yro. Especially when things got bad. I have seen things and did things any 5yro should have never experienced. I can recall waking up alone crying in the middle of the night, wondering why my mother have tricked me again by saying she was going to come right back to bed. I will find her high on crack in our bathroom instead. She will show me how talented she was by leaning so far from the toilet without falling. I remember watching her black silk skin glisten as sweat poured down her face as her high took her to another world. I guess she wanted to escape our empty home as well. Even with her being high, our eyes connected and sung the same song. It seems as if her eyes smiled at me telling me she's away right now but will be back soon. I will usually leave her in the bathroom until she comes back from her high vacation. These were the days my eyes have encountered. Then there were days when I became a hunter. I remember learning how to climb the kitchen counter so I can find some food in the cabinet when no one else was home. I was home alone often; however, my mother taught me how to survive. I learned quickly how to stand on my tippy toes as my 5yro hands will reach to the highest cabinet, searching for something to ease the hunger pains. I will do as my mother taught me and grab water and sugar to satisfy my sweet cravings. When my mother will leave, she will leave me my favorite meal: rice and hot chocolate. These days were usual for me. Having little to no food was our norm. I guess it's the reason why I appreciate food now. I remember feeling the silence in our project apartment and the only thing that kept me feeling alive were the police sirens outside our window. Silence started to scare me, so hearing any sounds allowed me to feel like I EXISTED. One would have thought I was the only child the way I lived. I lived with one sister and two brothers who were all older than me. But age didn't mean anything. In that house, we were all lost. In that house, our eyes created our own survival individually. Unfortunately, it left me alone most of the time.

I remember my siblings being in the house. Nothing more. No sister and brother arguments, no sister and brother play time not even a "I love you".

I do remember my 2nd oldest brother laughing at me for crying, when I saw my mother get arrested for the first time. I also remember my sister yelling at me because I was crying for my mom, late at night once. I was 7yro.

Oddly, I don't remember my other brother and I relationship. He was the oldest out of us three and was always on the move. So yeah, I recall a lot of memories as a child. Mostly bad ones. However, I recall having an imagination like no other. Most days and nights my imagination would save me. I called it: "My imagination friend" and we would get lost as hours passes by. My imagination became my protection. It was something I grew to love even when my mom wasn't there to give me the love I needed.

You see my mom, went by the name by Ms. G. and always had a tough skin for life. Being Puerto Rican with dark skin, and nappy hair has been a challenge for her while growing up. Everywhere she went people would question her race and look confused whenever she spoke Spanish or said her name out loud, "Gladys Escalera". As if that wasn't challenging enough, seeing her father abuse her mother, caused my mom to be the protector of the family. Sadly, it also has caused her anger to grow into violence and slipped into drugs. From fighting our neighbors to shooting dope, my mom grew a reputation and yet her smile and generous heart, captivated people. Throughout her whole life, she always tried to help someone before helping herself. Unfortunately, while she tried to save the world from drowning, she never checked for holes in her own boat. I can go on and on about the life events that drove my mother into killing herself, but this book is not about that. This book is about

    B-A-L-A-N-C-E.

A word I've learned from my survival journey. Like creating a reader and an author to connect on a level they both didn't expected to. This is not a poetry book or a book only about my life. This book is for US. It's about seeing yourself underneath my skin. It's about taking yourself on a journey to embrace your pains because it gave you strength to keep going and led you to seek healing. It's about letting go of "going through" so you can grow through the cleansing stage. Here is my life:

Life Growing up:

I grew up in the ghetto projects in Brooklyn, NY called "Farragut Houses", where survival was the second thing to breathing. However, as a child, none of this mattered… not yet at least. Everyone knew me because of the reputation my family have had. My oldest brother, Mikey, had a million-dollar smile and charm that will make anyone do anything. He was humbled, kind and highly respected but had an anger most have feared. He kept it cool and discreet. My second oldest brother, Andrew, was a hot head. He was always ready for war and yet had a lot of females drooling over him. He had a sense of humor everyone loved, and he made everyone felt like family.

My sister, Lexi, was what every man wanted. She had long black silky hair, oval shaped eyes, nice body and a beautiful heart. She also was filled with painful secrets. My sister tried her best being a mom figure to me since she was 11yro whenever our mother was too busy being high as a kite in the streets. Looking from the outside in, you would have thought we were well put together but inside we were dying slowly. We were all affected by our mother's way of living, but we learned how to survive.

    I remember, every day, I would get up with an imagination that, that day will be full of adventures. The hallway in our apartment would be a slip and slide while the kitchen, living room and bathroom were my jungle gym. Underneath the bed was my cave and every table or dresser in that apartment were mountains. I was ready to explore what to me, was the unknown. A few times, however, on a good day, my mom would even entertain my wild thoughts and will pretend to be the monster who tries to hunt "the wild explorer." She would then become a nature goddess and tell me everything she knew about the "winds of life". We would be cuddled up in the bed creating adventure stories full of laughter and light. She made sure each story she told had valuable lessons. I always seem to get lost in her stories. I swear if I stared long enough, I would be able to see the magic glow that radiates in her eyes looking back at me. As if there was a child in there smiling. These days, I held onto tightly, until night fall. That's when reality would hit and the person that birthed me usually become someone else.

This particular time wasn't a good one. I remember waking up one night seeing my mom go from crying to yelling in anger. It was about not finding cigarettes, but I knew it was more than that. My mom's emotions would become irrational when she didn't catch her high when she wanted it. I often saw myself as my mom's savior. When she was sad, I will do anything to make her smile. If she was upset, I will agree with however she felt that day. She will play me against my siblings, and I was ok with it for a little while. I mean, at least I got some attention in that empty house. At 6 years old, I started to understand who I was becoming, and it left me confused.

I will find myself walking into rooms unintentionally, where sex filled the air. I remember one room specifically. I was at my mother's friend house and I was looking for a toy to play with. I didn't think twice to knock before walking in. Red walls from the red light grabbed my attention. As I heard music playing, my eyes became captivated with the two bodies on the bed. The slow music and the moans from the bed made me feel like I was watching a movie that was forbidden and I became numb. Watching a man dominating a female while she grabs him like he's the last thing on Earth, I just knew what I was watching was wrong and yet I was stuck. My mind was screaming for me to leave but my feet wouldn't move. My mom's friend, Maria grabbed me, slammed the door and told me to never walk in a room without knocking first. At the age of 6, I learned was sex was and I liked it. I was always with Maria. My mom will leave me with her friends often, so I knew how to adapt to strangers rather quickly.

    I was told that my name, Diana means "goddess of the moon". Such a contradiction to be named something representing night when that's the very thing I feared most. Nighttime was the worst for me. It's when I felt the loneliest.

It's when I felt like I was being watched by every horror movie I've seen. It's when my mom will throw a party, get drunk and "mothered" drugs at home while I am forced to be put to bed early. It's when strange hands will wipe off their sins on my skin when my mother wasn't looking. It's when screaming became silence and nothing happens, and no one listens. It's when all hell breaks loose, and the demons reclaim their thrones. It's when I learned that silence has become the loudest noise this world has ignored. Nighttime was indeed the worst for me, and the darkness knew I was afraid of it.

I remember a special day. It was my birthday. I was turning 7yro. Kids were running around and having fun and I wore the same pink fluffy silky dress I had for years. That's how we did it in my family. Wore clothing that were passed down from someone else or wear the same clothing for years.

Either way, I felt happy. My mom was being the life of the party as usual. Music was blasting, food and beers surrounding my home, and everyone was having a good time. It seemed like my birthday party lasted forever- until it became an adult party. It was getting late, hours have passed, and I was getting sleepy. People were still dancing but to a slower beat. My brothers and sister were not around, all the kids went home, and my mom was in the living room having her 5th beer. I honestly wanted everyone to go home so I can have my mom's attention all to myself. I guess she had other plans.

I came into the living room and sat down on the couch trying to stay up for my mother, but my eyes were getting heavy. "Mamita, you can lay down in the room if you're tired", my mom said. "No, I'm not sleepy", I lied. I just wanted to be around her and enjoy her company. She then asked her male friend to pick me up and take me to the room while she followed. Being placed in a dark room, at a young age for bed and seeing your mom walk away without any hugs or kisses goodnight to entertain the bodies that took over your home instead, does something to a child's mind. I don't know why, but I cried. All I kept saying to myself was "Why doesn't she love me enough to stay?" "Why can't she just make everyone leave?" Even with music and laughter blasting outside my mom's room where I slept, I couldn't help but feel like death was with me, watching me lay. Darkness always found a way to taunt me. I tried very hard to sleep that night, but my tears wouldn't let me.

Looking back at it now, I guess that's why I am not fond of the darkness.

Healing Time

Have you ever had a flash back or a memory that popped into your mind during an unusual time? How did you feel? What did you do? These blank pages are for YOUR story and to understand that your SURVIVAL is yours. Not someone else's. Its ok to be vulnerable here.

_____

_____

_____

_____

_____

_____

EYE SURVIVED

EYE SURVIVED

EYE SURVIVED

EYE CHANGED

I was 14 years old. I was in my tomboy stage rocking a side ponytail to show that I have a slight girly side about me. At this point of life, I wasn't sure how I saw myself. Looking at my two best friends, Donna and Casey, I knew I didn't fit in their caliber. Donna was slim, with long legs cinnamon skin and pretty, brown eyes. Her shy personality attracted boys to her. Casey, who had a vanilla pecan skin tone had what most will call a "coke-shaped bottle figure". Long hair, pretty contacts and the sweetest voice had everyone drooling over her, even me. With my short frame, hairy arms and legs, long chin, big forehead and boyish style, I was always looked at as one of the "homeboys", but I didn't mind. We were planning to go to hang out at "Fort Greene projects", another ghetto neighborhood across the street to see some of our friends. Our usual day to day activities. Honestly, it started to bore me. We will go over there with our cute outfits, joke around with the boys and have fun. Donna and Casey will usually be split up with their "boy crush" while I sit there, sometimes playing basketball by myself or just talking to one of my friends.

I watched how Donna and Casey flirt with the boys. "Girl, I know they're being nasty over there", giggled Jean. "They been over there in front of that building for a long time, knowing we're right here waiting for them".

Jean was a cool, down to earth, don't test her kind of chick. She knew everyone and always got respected. She had big breast, thick thighs and an attractive personality and she knew how to fight. Jean taught me how the boys were in this hood. She wasn't the type of girl that can be played. I felt safe with Jean. I always find myself staying behind and talking to her. I learned a lot from watching her. I'll be damn if I got played by any boy in this hood.

Donna, Casey and the boys, K-Dot and C-LO, walk over to us. "Wassup up with tonight?" asked K-Dot. "We about to go over to Jah house and chill". His best friend C-LO chimed in. "Word, our homeboy bringing drinks and smoke, you should come through". I wasn't a smoker yet, but the smell of weed always sparked my curiosity. I've been drinking since 8yro, so beer and liquor was a norm to me, thanks to my mother when she kept me out late nights. "Aight, I'm down", I nervously said. I wanted to be seen. Not as a tomboy but as a girly girl. I looked up to Donna and Casey because they always got the attention I lowkey craved for. Sometimes, I even pretended to like a boy. It was hard though, knowing I had weird feelings about my sexuality and keeping it a secret. As my friends were talking, I couldn't help but notice another female walking by and something about her walk and the way her hips moved, excited me. I asked Jean, "who dat?" as my eyes was stuck on her as she walked. Jean was too busy talking to the boys. "Damn" I said to myself. This girl had on blue leggings and a crop top shirt. She walked with a bounce, so everything was moving. As I watched her, a memory flashed in front of my eyes:

(**Memory**)

It was late. I got up from the couch and made sure everyone was sleep. I knew I shouldn't have been awake, but the magazines were calling me. I went into my mom's private draw and quietly took out the "Playboy" mag. I knew there was a chance I will get caught, but my 8yro mind didn't care. I did this often so what's the odds of getting caught? I hurried back to the couch and flipped through the pages in the magazine slowly. I grew excited. My eyes were in a trance as each page were turned. I liked what I saw, and I couldn't figure out why. My heartbeat beat a little faster and throbbing took place between my legs. I thought I heard my mom call my name, so I hurried and put the magazines back.

(Memory fades)

"DIANA!" "Girl, I've been calling you for a minute now" said Jean. "Donna and Casey just went upstairs with K-Dot and C-LO". "Are you coming?" Still thinking about my memory, I said, "yeah, I'm coming." As soon as we got off the elevator, the smell of weed filled the air. When we walked in, everyone had a cup in their hand and a blunt was being passed around. They were playing a game and they called it "CHICAGO". It's when you stand in a circle, take a pull off the blunt, hold the smoke in your mouth without swallowing until it's your turn to smoke again. But I didn't know any of this until now. "What are they doing?" I asked. "Girl, you smoke and never heard of Chicago?" K-Dot teased. "It gives you a bigger High". "No, I heard it, I just never actually played it". I lied again. Everyone laughed. Feeling embarrassed, I took the blunt and pulled hard. I held it for seconds which felt like minutes and exhaled. My body instantly felt light and the room got hazy. Within minutes, I felt like I wasn't in my body. It was scary but intriguing. I took 2 more pulls, sat down and started to play spades with other people that were in the apartment.

Within an hour, I found myself walking to the bathroom wishing that I could be sober. I felt like I was floating. My stomach started to feel weird. I kept asking myself "Why did I play that stupid game?" As I was making my way down the hall towards the bathroom, I saw a room with bunk beds. I peeked in and there was another girl having sex. Door wide open, lights on and she was loud. Watching her grab the bed sheets as he grabs her skin pounding away her innocence, I became numb. I watched her face expression. Her body wanted him, but her eyes were empty. Either way, he didn't stop. I wanted to turn away and leave, but another memory flashed before my eyes.

(**Memory**)

I was 14 years old. I remember it was late because it was past my curfew. I just finished hanging out with my friend Lilly in Farragut. I was messed up from drinking Hennessy all night. I planned to stay overnight at her house, so I could sober up by the morning. I didn't want my sister to find out I was drinking.

I was in the elevator laughing and walking drunk trying to look sober, but people had already seen me that night. I came into Lilly's apartment, and passed out in the spare room. I woke up in the middle of the night feeling very heavy, to the point I couldn't breathe. When I opened my eyes, there he was. Like a lion who hasn't eaten in days he was sweaty, putting all his body weight on top of me sucking on my barely developed breast pressing his teeth into my skin. At first, I thought I was dreaming, since it was very similar to the nightmares I once had in my younger years. But I wasn't. This was real. This was happening to me, now. I scanned the room, but it was too dark for me to see. I still felt drunk and weak. I sat there at first quiet. Hearing his grunts and the sound of his saliva dripping on my skin. I became numb.

I tried slowly to push him off. Feeling confused and dizzy, I thought to myself. Maybe he thought I was another girl? Maybe he was too drunk to notice I was only 14yro? Maybe this was a mistake. He didn't budge as my hands slowly but sternly tried to push him off again. I whispered, "Please stop." "Get off me please." I felt like I was losing my voice. He just grunted and kept sucking and gripping my skin. My breast started to hurt. He looked at me, twice and went back to it. Even in the dark, his eyes were so dull. No life in it. I closed my eyes, wishing a good memory will pop up this time, but my mind failed me. This nightmare seemed to last forever. I felt like throwing up as the bed rocked from the weight of us. I wanted it to all stop.

Fortunately, Lilly's Mom walked in and yelled, "Boy what are you doing in this room?" "Get out and go to your own damn room!" She walked out angrily. He got up, threw the blanket on me as if he was covering a dead body and left the room. The door closed behind him and I exhaled. I looked around and saw darkness laugh at me while I began to sink into the bed. "Did she notice him on top of me?" "Why didn't she come back to see if I was ok?" "Am I that invisible?" Questions after questions flooded my brain. I prayed that I could just disappear. I felt like I didn't exist, and my tears were too afraid to water my dry body. I didn't know what to think. I tried hard not to think. For some odd reason, I kept repeating "It didn't happen" over and over until I fell asleep.

(Memory fades)

While standing in the door seeing the girl get pounded out in the room I snapped back into reality. "I'm so sorry, I have the wrong room" I said. I went into the bathroom, splashed water on my face, pretended to use the bathroom and walked out with a new attitude. I wasn't going to let anyone take control over me like that ever again. I won't be afraid to do what my other friends are doing, and I will be the best at it. I was tired of being looked at as weak. I was done with being "invisible".

I walked into the living room, grabbed K-Dot, took him into the same room with the bunk beds and got on the top bunk and stared at him. I can tell he was shocked. "Yo, you good?" he laughed. "Yeah, come here". I replied. The bottom bunk was still occupied but that didn't stop us from making our own music. I was still a virgin, so I know I wasn't going to go all the way, but I was going to get pretty, darn close. During those 20 minutes, I learned two things: Never be afraid to take control and know that men love a submissive woman. So, I submitted. I allowed my body to be his playground and I got lost. Between being high and drunk I felt like I was on a roller coaster. Enjoying a ride, I never wanted to get on, but something about being scared caused me to become curious. I also learned a new trick. Being seductive in an innocent way will get you what you want in life. Thus, a flirty personality was born.

HEALING TIME

Have you ever been in a situation where you found yourself changing for the worse? Sometimes, certain situations and people around us can affect how we think and go about things. Tell me a time where you saw yourself start to change. What did you notice?

_____

_____

_____

_____

_____

_____

_____

EYE SURVIVED

EYE SURVIVED

HEALING TIME

What we see in our lifetime shapes the character we become. Name some things that your eyes have experience that has become a trigger for you now. How do you deal with them? How does it make you feel? It's ok to not have answers to everything. This is the space and time to release all your feelings here:

_____

_____

_____

_____

_____

_____

EYE SURVIVED

EYE SURVIVED

EYE SURVIVED

LESSONS EYE WILL NEVER FORGET

When I wasn't hanging out with my friends, I was at home facing reality of life. From picking my mother up off the streets because she got too drunk to come home, to coming home with no food in the fridge and seeing crack heads taking over the apartment. From seeing my mother kick my siblings out leaving me behind, to seeing her cry herself to sleep. There have been times when I would come home and be reminded of how much my siblings sacrificed their life for me or stories of how I was the lucky one because I didn't get beat until blood came out of me. What no one knew is that I would rather have taken those whippings then to wake up to an empty home every day and sleep alone every night not knowing when the next time I will get a hug or a "I love you" or even a conversation that lasted longer than 5 minutes. I went from being ok with it to being frustrated with my mom and the way she chose her life. This was my first lesson I've learned. Nobody has to care. Not even your own blood.

Then there were times I will admire her. I remember walking behind the projects in DUMBO one day, and I saw my mom by herself, on some street with a can of beer, drawing. I never allowed her to see me, however, I watched. I watched how she was in silence. I watched how her cries poured out on paper creating beautiful art and I watched the little girl in her who never got to feel what real love was. I was learning why she was tough. I was learning why she hurt and why she hid so much dirt underneath her nails. Her spirit talked through her drawings and it was like I was the only person in the world who could see it. She taught me vividly how much of a "Bitch" you must be in life. How love came with a price and how no man is a good man. She even taught me how to hold my emotions in and to always fight against the bad in life. Granted, these lessons weren't always the right way to be taught but she loved me the best she knew how.

Her voice is clear as day still. "Diana, don't you get knock down and if you do, you get up and whoop ass". That stood with me until this day. My mother was strong in her weakness. Even when she was high on drugs, she always tried to protect her other high friends. She either fought their battles or fed them. I understand why she did what she did now, but back then, it was creating a monster within me. These lessons I learned were a gift and a curse. It helped me see the world in a different way. A way that most people wouldn't agree with. I didn't see the bad. I just saw the hurt in people eyes unfortunately, nothing phased me. That was the curse. Emotions were nowhere to be found and I was ok with that. As I watched my mother empty her pains through her pencil from a distance, a memory flashed before my eyes:

(Memory)

I was coming from the store with a bag of salt n vinegar chips in my hand. As I was walking across the street, I saw my mother walking towards me. "Here we go" I whispered to myself. My mother was always in the street getting high or fighting somebody. Something was different about her today though. Her face was filled with worry and her walk was unsure. "Hey Ma" I said, not really caring what she had to say. "Diana, I have to tell you something". Hearing her voice crack made me drop my attitude. She sat me down with tears in her eyes and said, "I got AIDS". I immediately thought, "of course you do, you get high on crack" looking at me as if she can read my thoughts she responded, " I didn't get it from getting high, I had sex with John and he didn't tell me he had AIDS".

John was a nice guy. I didn't know much about him, but I knew he lived with his children. I came to call his family my family. He always smiled, always was kind to me and he made my mom happy. I sat quietly. I felt like I was in a movie. What's the odd of someone hooked on drugs and yet, get AIDS through sex instead. I stared at my mother's sad face. I felt like screaming but nothing came out. I watched how the glow from her black skin slip into darkness. She started to cry. She kept saying "Sorry" over and over again. I felt my throat started to get dry. No. I wasn't going to cry, not now. Not ever. I got up and said these words, I soon will regret: "You are sorry, and you never loved me." She cried. I felt horrible but I couldn't show her my weakness. She taught me that. To stand strong even when you want to fall. I walked away, knowing that will be the day I turned my back on my own mom.

(Memory fades)

I snapped back into reality and finish watching my mom draw. I wanted to run over there and hug her, love on her and tell her I'm sorry. I couldn't. My pain wouldn't allow me to, so I walked away.

HEALING TIME

What are some of life lessons you will never forget? What has caused these life lessons to occur? How do you use these life lessons in your life now? Have these life lessons helped or hurt you? Sometimes we forget the lessons in life that taught us how to survive. Express yourself freely below.

_____

_____

_____

_____

_____

_____

_____

EYE SURVIVED

EYE SURVIVED

EYE SURVIVED

EYE HAVE GOOD NEWS

I was a freshman at Boys and Girl High school in Brooklyn, NY. Around this time, I was aware of my feelings about girls and still had unknown feelings about boys. Everyone knew me as a dancer. Most people thought I dance for fun, when actually, I dance to escape this world momentarily. It was my escape from life, my safe space. It was my drug. Seeing so much growing up, I developed a thick skin. I mastered having a vibrant personality, a flirty attitude with a mean streak. Dancing allowed me to feel free.

What I didn't master was looking pretty. I still didn't get noticed by any boys and if I did, they became my homies. As for females, I became their protector. It was easy for me to get a female to trust me. I felt like I had to save them from anything that may cause them harm. I was still cool enough to get friends. Being 16yro was semi-fun. At this time, I lived with my sister. I hung out with my friends, went to an afterschool program called "Dr. White" where I received stipends for good behavior amongst other things and I tried my best to laugh, a lot. It was at Dr. White when I notice how bad my anger was. I was already attending anger management classes until 2004 at Dr. White so I knew my anger needed some guidance. I saw a counselor once a week and attended to all their workshops. They all treated me good here. It was like I was able to get a new family and start over in my life. These were the good days.

    I remember it was March 2004, I was now 17yro. I was on my way to Donna's house to see if we can hang out after school. While waiting for Donna to get dress, her mom handed me the phone. "Um, Diana this is for you" "He said he's your father". I just stared at the phone in confusion. "What?" "I haven't seen or heard from "my father", since I was a newborn" I chuckled. I listened quietly on the phone waiting to hear the voice that created me. "Diana?" This is your Dad." I froze. "I have your brother Joey right here to confirm that it's really me." I immediately ask for Joey. "Hey sis, can't you believe it?!" "Dad got out of jail and is now staying in Virginia" "He wants to see you and make everything right again." Joey is my half-brother that I tried to keep connections with throughout the years. Joey sounded excited. I couldn't believe what I was hearing. I didn't know what to feel. So, I did what I knew what to do best. I became another person. "Aww that's awesome!" "Here's my number." "I will call you later, so we can talk more." I just wanted to get off the phone and get lost. Donna and I left her house and I made sure that day drinking, and smoking became my best friends.

I woke up the next morning with a hangover and an attitude. 'Who he thinks he is coming into my life like that" I thought to myself. "I have never spoken to him and I don't even remember how he looks!" I became angry. I threw my phone, screamed into the pillow so my sister wouldn't hear and made my knuckles catch the brunt of my anger. Besides a small cut on knuckle, my hand was ok, but my dresser wasn't. I felt lost again. After crying silently, I wiped my face, put on my smile for the day and walked out to hang with my friends.

After a few weeks since the call, I have spoken to my father 3 times. Asking so many questions of why he went to jail, how was my mom and his relationship, and what was I like as a newborn. He was so eager to know me again and to see me while I just wanted information from him and nothing more. After speaking to my father, I considered maybe giving him a chance. I wondered. "Who goes searching for their daughter after 17 years and begs them to meet them?" I started to have daydreams of what it would be like to just see him, laugh with him and hold him. I made a scary decision. I was going to meet, the man that helped create me.

EYE NEVER THOUGHT EYE SEE THE DAY

I have told my counselor and friends about getting the call from my dad and speaking to him to get answers. They were all happy and supportive of me. I was happy again. Working on my grades in school, getting help with my anger and being surrounded by people who cared about me. Things were looking up. My mom wasn't feeling too well so she was taken to the hospital. I've seen her the night she was admitted for a few minutes, but I wanted to see her again, so I left school early trying to see my mother at the hospital this morning, but I wasn't allowed to. I wanted to give her the good news about my dad finding me and tell her about Dr. White. I was determined to allow happiness in my life no matter how complex it gets. Feeling like new beginnings, I started to become better with handling my anger however, life has a funny way of taking you back to reality, because today May 19th was the day, I received the worst news ever.

My counselor sat me down. She sat in front of me with tears falling down her face as she prepared me for the devastating news. "I'm sorry, but your brother wanted me to tell you that your mom has died." Once I heard it, my heart sunk, and it finally hit me. They wouldn't let me see my mom because she was gone already. I dazed out and that's when a memory of my mom on Mother's Day flashed in front of my eyes.

(Memory)

Mother's Day 2004. It was a weekend. My family and I was at grandma's house. I was hanging out with this guy I liked that became my best friend. The plan was to go to Grandma's house, say hi then leave. I wasn't big on hanging around family growing up as a teen. I saw how much they never really tried to help us. Help me. I guess you can say life has showed me that family isn't always family. We saw each other but mostly on holidays. You know, tradition routines. So, it wasn't like they really cared. I remember walking in, and everyone was excited to see me. While my arms were being occupied by exercising every hug, my eyes shift the room quickly to see if my mother was able to make it. It's been a couple of weeks since I've seen my mom. The last incident didn't go so well. I think she was upset with me because I cursed the drug dealer out for making her beg for what they call in the street "Candy". I had a surprise for her to make up what for I've done. I asked my grandma. "Is mommy here?". My grandma's joyous spirit was slowly fading away as I waited for the answer. "Yes, she's in the room but she needs to be alone for a little, she's ok though." I didn't believe her.

I quickly went to my grandma's room and saw that my mom was facing the window, sitting on the bed. "Happy Mother's Day Ma!" I said, trying to be excited. She loved this holiday. She would always cry when I would make a card or tell her how much I love her on this day when I was younger. But no response. "Ma?" I walked around the bed and stared at my mother. That was the first time I saw an empty soul. My mother's dark skin was inflating. Like a balloon with a slow leak, my mom face was disappearing right in front of me and I didn't know how to breathe life back into her. "Ma, you ok?" Again, no response. I sat down with her. I had her Mother's Day gift in a plastic bag. I took out what I had. "Look Ma, I got your favorite." I pulled out a banana, orange slices candy and socks. I didn't have much, but this is what she loved. Finally, she moved. She slowly turned her head towards my way and stared at me. There goes that darkness again. Laughing. It now has her. It was like the devil himself took over. "Ma, you ok?" I nervously asked. Still, nothing. I quickly heard her voice in my head. "Stay strong baby."

I kept talking about the gifts I bought her hoping to hear her raspy voice I missed so much. I immediately felt like I had to let her know how much I missed her. I put her things near the window and sat closer. I kissed her cheeks, hugged her, told her I loved her and just kept smiling. "My smile will make her say something" I thought to myself. Still nothing. I told her I will be right back. I got up, feeling sick to my stomach. I walked out the room calmly. "What's wrong with mommy?" I asked everyone in the living room. It was like everyone knew but no one said much. My grandmother spoke again. "She's going to be ok." I started to get upset. "Why does this family keep secrets and act like I don't have the right to be told the truth?" I thought to myself. "I'm leaving" I said. My friend who was with me just gave me the "You ready" look and we left. I couldn't deal with the overflowing thoughts that filled my head. I felt anxious. I felt upset. I felt sad. I haven't cried for so long, but I knew my tears were there, hiding somewhere, waiting for me to let it out. So instead, I smoked. I allowed the drug to take over me so that I won't have to live… in the moment. I just kept seeing my mom eyes. Looking through me, like she wasn't there. He took her. The devil finally took my mother.

That night I got a call from my sister telling me our mother was in the hospital. I wasn't sure what to think or how to feel. I met everyone at the hospital in Brooklyn, NY. I walked in only wanting to see one person, my mom. Never in a million years would I have pictured by mom being hooked up to different IV's and being told we can't touch her without gloves. The room was so small. I looked at my sister and within minutes they were ready to go. I couldn't leave yet, so I told them I was staying behind just for a little bit longer.

Once my mother's room door was closed, I took off my gloves and touched her hand and squeezed it. I asked her what happened and why is this happening. I didn't get a response. I then got mad and said these exact words: "You always said you was tired, and you can't do this anymore, but you have to stay here for one more day, just one more, so I can see you before you go." That was the first time I saw her eyes open since I been in that room. I knew she heard me. I knew it was her time.

I told her she couldn't leave me because I wouldn't know what to do.

(Memory fades)

I snapped back to the room, where I saw my counselor mouthing some words -her voice started to become clear to me. "Are you ok Diana?" I smiled. Not because I was happy, but because I already knew deep down in my heart my mom wasn't going to make it and to hear a stranger give me the news that my own blood couldn't share with me was amusing to me. I got up and called my oldest brother. He met me at Dr. White, and we sat in a private room. "What time did she die?" I asked. He looked at me. "12:15pm" he said. I thought to myself "She tried to hold on, but I was too late". Within minutes I pretended I was ok. I dismissed my brother and started to make my way to one of the workshops that was happening at Dr. White. I guess my spirit had other plans. As soon as I walked in the room, I felt darkness upon my skin. My heart started racing and tears filled my eyes. I flipped tables, screamed, punched, yelled, cursed and hollered at the top of my lungs until my throat was on fire. I ended my melt down with screaming the words "You left me!!" "You left me by myself!" "Why did you leave me!" I was 17yro. That's when my life ended emotionally, mentally and spiritually.

PAIN WASN'T DONE WITH ME

My mother passed away May 19th, 2004. Since her death for many years, life has taken its toll on me. I have gone through depression like it was my favorite drink. I received a call that my father got into a car accident in Virginia a month and some days after my mom's death. My father died in June of 2004, before I even got the chance to see him. I soon fell into a domestic violence relationship, couldn't keep a job long enough, ended up pregnant and dreamt of suicide like it was my favorite dream in the world. I was full of anger, sadness and lots of fake smiles. I wore the face many people walk around with today. I was a walking corpse. I was mothering a baby girl name Carmen while I was motherless. I always felt like my daughter didn't deserve to live with someone who was lost. I had no sense of direction but to keep going even when I tried to take myself out. I didn't know why I was still living. I didn't understand my purpose and what it meant. I just knew I was existing.... for nothing, so I believed.

Then in 2009, my world became darker than it has ever been. Still being involved in an abusive relationship, he planted another child in me. By 4 months my son was diagnosed with Trisomy 18. His name was Khaliel and he lived for 2 months once I gave birth. He spent all his time in a hospital where I remember having endless nights of crying and watching my son die. By this time, the devil had me by the throat. March 2009 and March 2010, I was robbed twice in 2 different boroughs. Both where my life could have ended and yet I survived. Then April 2010, I had a spinal surgery which doctors told me I wasn't going to dance like how I used to. Coming out of surgery made me hate my life and where it was. I became addicted to pain pills, I tried fulfilling myself with multiple partners and I went from shelter to shelter like I owned the buildings. I was a lost soul, looking for any place called home. My last straw was when I tried to overdose on pills in 2011 and woke up fine. I was baffled. I was angry. I was confused. Why haven't I died? A question that remained in my head for a long time.

PAIN IS ONLY TEMPORARILY

That was the first time I cried out to God. I wasn't into any religion or went to churches but calling on him was my last option. I wanted to know if GOD was really real.

Then a miracle happened.

November 2011, a God serving woman who held the spirit of my mom with a loving soul reached out to me. She was my daughter's grandfather's wife. I didn't have much relationship with my daughter's father side of the family, but She helped my daughter and I move out of New York to Baltimore, MD. From the big city lights to quiet street lights with a block full of houses. An environment I never thought I would see myself in. Of course, just like everything else in life, this was a process. A healing process for my daughter and me. I never cried so hard on so many nights feeling afraid of the change I made and feeling uncomfortable with the whole idea of starting over and not knowing what will happen if I do.

I just knew my back was against the wall and I was suffocating slowly. What else can I go through? From being abandon at 5 years old to being abandon as a grown woman I wasn't afraid of anything anymore. I have been through the fire, got burnt and went through it again. I knew all about the heat from life, so moving to Maryland was my last attempt. It was the best, scariest, bravest, craziest, thing I have ever done, and I don't regret not one thing about this journey.

I have been in Maryland since 2011 and counting and I have encountered blessings and lessons here. Nothing compared to where I came from and for that I will forever be grateful. During my time here, I have encountered so many beautiful souls that also walk the journey I have walked or are currently walking their journey. I've seen pieces of me in everyone eyes. I still had a bumpy road for a few years in Maryland, but my roads were becoming smoother day by day. It confirmed my purpose of helping those who need to be seen emotionally, mentally and spiritually. I became at peace. I started to release my pains and traumas into art. I fell in love with poetry and music. Never in a million years I would have thought I will be here. Here is where my life began.

So, let me tell you. I see you. The you who hide so well from the world. No, I really, really see you. I thank you. For existing. For breathing. For…. Surviving. Life isn't easy and it wasn't meant to be. Life is meant to shape you, mold you and polish you into the person you were born to be, even when it hurts.

Remember, you are on this journey not for YOU. As crazy as that may seem. Understand that the journey you are on, is for the lost souls who is looking for the footprints that survived his or her story. I have survived. I have died my old ways to relive a better life. You are a survivor. If you were able to wake up and survived your yesterdays, you are a survivor. If you are reading this and going through this healing journey with me, you are a survivor! You are living this life that can help and save thousands even millions of people who is looking for someone that can relate to their journey. I am proud of you. I am thankful that you and I get to heal and survive together. Please don't ever dare give up! Fight the good fight and keep going!

HEALING TIME

Right here, right now I want you to understand that the events that have happened or are currently happening in your life don't have to stop you from healing and moving forward. Big or small you do not have to allow anything to have control over your life without your permission. You can ALWAYS turn a negative into a positive. Below I want you to vent. Vent anything that you are feeling from reading my story or from anything that you may have been going through. When you are done writing, I want you to end your sentence with this quote "I will not be led, by the things I've seen, instead I will lead with the lessons it brings".

EYE SURVIVED

EYE SURVIVED

EYE SURVIVED

EYE SURVIVED

EYE SURVIVED

From quotes to poetry, I hope you enjoy these next following pages!

Write Your Own Quote with me!

"Without a reader, there is no story"

"_____

_____"

"How can you move forward with no feet? Simple, you CRAWL"

"_____

_____"

"Life is like a balance beam, slim path with many distractions and yet when you fall you can always try again"

"_____

_____ "

"Love and pain cannot live without each other, how else would you know what they are if you haven't experience one of the other?"

"_____

_____ "

"To be, or not to be a lesson...for someone or for yourself"

"_____

_____ "

"Even the rainbow wasn't trying to be great, it just was"

"_____

_____"

"Survival is surviving your yesterdays even when you feel dead inside"

"_____

_____"

"Your hugs weren't just mean for other people, they were meant for you as well"

"_____

_____"

POETRY OF LIFE

SHATTERED

She was tagged with a price.... a price no pockets will be willing to afford. She sat on the top shelf with other items that were spread abroad.

She felt valuable.... someone special who can afford her will buy her......soon...so she thought...

She made sure she looked perfect so that she can be brought, but maturity was not taught so various types of attention she always sought

Weeks turn into months and months turned into years and she still stood there wondering why no one seem to care to pay what she cost....

And now she feels lost.....as dust seem to film over her canvas the label "trash" was now tagged to the price that was now tossed to a discounted number.....cheap...she became. .at this point, she is just yearning for any man.

She finally came in contact with her buyer.... his mouth was no match to his heart, but she grew a custom to this liar, his money satisfied her desires...because she was born with a worth that can be brought. He became her sire...and she became really tired, but she did everything for him to prevent her from getting fired for she was afraid he might do a new hire and she would be back...on the top shelf.... with dust over her canvas...at a price that was cheap....

He grew strong as she grew weak... he lived in free while she waits to get beat. His money was his safe.... if she got paid then it wasn't called rape.... she became loose like a pair of shoelaces.

While he keeps her quiet by throwing stacks in her face...she felt lower than the gum at the bottom of her heels...a number.... soon was a numb to her because she failed to feel...now she never looks in the mirror for all she knows was that she was placed on the shelf....

But today was the day for the first time she will see herself...

He once told her she was a package that was too good to be open...but rigid lines she felt on her body that no longer were gloating, so she did the unspoken.

She looked into the mirror.... she stood there....in shocked... now realizing why it took so long to be brought.... she now understands why he said:

"I'm the only one that's willing to have her"...because she was nothing but used puzzle pieces that were once shattered.

SHOW MORE, GIVE LESS

He says...Show more...give less.... show more give less. He says. show more intelligence that I can read from your mind than the cleavage that comes from your chest. Don't just give away straight A's let em earn their passing grade to this test. Show more finesse...let a man want to yearn to find your treasure chest. ...don't just serve yourself on a paper plate...or do simple tricks of how far your legs can separate don't create this trait.... don't be that woman that's just another bait doesn't be that female who's just another pretty face.... don't let this be your fate. All meals may look good but not all have a great taste.

A woman who walks with grace wore this silky lace type of dress...fine as she was swaying her hips from right to left, she tried to seduce these guys with her sexiness.... but there was one who caught her eye she addresses by putting her hands slightly on his chest -he leans over and whispered. ...I rather see your naked mind then what's between your thighs try harder next time...

I rather if you had showed some more and give less but instead you told every nigga he won by wearing this see through dress my lady you're a girl in disguise trapped in a woman's big breast and a round behind. .and I'm not surprised. he said you have such beauty in your eyes but you came here to complete a mission and that's to seek those who won't remember you when it hits sunrise...

So ladies...it's cool to dress up pretty or pretty sexy...just show more of your soul than how much dick your pussy can hold, yes I'm speaking real shit so excuse my poem for being bold... but give more wonder to your precious secret...let a man go around the world for you before telling him he can keep it....now a days a hard base and dollar signs can make it an easy chase

..but things got to change. ...real women please take your stand...and let them know anyone can have sex.... but its best if you showed more and gave less.

WARRIOR

I've been tested... I've been pushed and pulled...I've been poked...teased and misunderstood. ...

I've been fighting since I was born unto this earth...

I've been beaten.... robbed and told I was nothing since birth

I been starved...alone and half complete. .

I've been in the wrong crowd.... walking behind the wrong types of feet. .

I've been lower than worms...yet I stride with my smile. ...I've been broken before and was called " wild".......

BUT MY GOD....look at the creation I am Now!! I've been standing every time the devil has tried to knock me down...I've grown to love genuinely and to live with peace... yes, I fight my demons daily. ...but with god it's definitely with ease...... I've changed my circumference. ...but still have friends .... people who I share my love with from day 1 to the end....

For you are too a Warrior! Trust me you are...because if I was wrong you would have not made it this far. ...you were able to skip death and woke up today. ...you were able to have a tongue and lips...use them to pray!

Look how god causes conversation and situations with you and another. ...no coincidence my friend. .... we must treat each other like sister and brothers. .

I am born to live like Jesus and die for my lord...as many deaths I saw my life he didn't abort.... So, I'm telling you Now...it's NEVER too late to get Happiness...Joy...and Peace ...

Because once I found God....he said he was waiting to set me free! I am now FREE!

HEAD HELD HIGH

They tried to hold me upside down so I can drown off my screaming sounds of my rights, but I keep my head held high.

They'll have to chained me down keep security around because I will not be another lost and found I will always fight. ...as I keep my head held high

I will let it be known that I am my own and not what they sold- truth be told, too many souls been towed and now the owners are going back to pick up their life... I'll still have my head held high
I'll have my head held so high that my thoughts would be unlimited like the sky......

I'll have my head held so high that my eyes will touch the sunlight... and the clouds will be rise...... they may try to break my knees because I declare I'm free and like Maya Angelou still I'll rise..

I'll rise above like a tidal wave conquering its waters strong I will proceed. ...I will stretch out my arms stick out my chest and declare that I love being me...I love the brown skin Puerto Rican I am.. who love gay men and lesbians that are not afraid to be who they want to be

I'll be strong like a lion who protect its breed. I will stand ground and proclaim my throne and succeed successfully as a noble queen.

Then I will teach my seed to live beautifully and that everything with growth can have beauty...

Every scenery has its own stories-every obstacle can have its own glory and that when she'll have a mind of bravery and the pursuit of her happy will be embedded

Like mending thread into gold everything she'll get a hold on will turn warm from its cold she will not catch a cold from this cold world she will have her armor vest to protect her heart in her chest she have her own helmet to protect her knowledge from becoming less- her shield will be her cover from hurt of the world that's against each other.. she will be left standing victoriously...outspoken...unbroken...spotless she will be....my princess next in line to be queen.... we ...will keep our heads held high.......

Until the day we close our eyes and even after. ...after our souls have taken flight.... the heavens will bless us with riches of everlasting happiness that has never been seen by mankind. Until then...I....her....my seed...we...will have our heads held high!

OPEN YOUR EYES

I see sad faces yet unchanged places, many angry voices crying out to black on black crime cases years go by and its unchanged phases- same story different headlines question mark on are we gonna make it? How long shall we fake it? Mad at the other race but were the ones hating our own races? Turning our backs on our neighbors… close mouths don't get fed so we eat off the pavement…

How about you open your eyes?

You seem more worried free when social media gives you just a little bit of taste and video clips on the new disease or black fights foolery got you glue to the screen but then a hash tag of #being free becomes more of a cliché then an identity.

How about you open your eyes?

I too, used to take the bait, wanted to be a part of something so I became close with friends like phony and fake but then I got really tired of that barbie food I used to take – yes, I learned. I've learned that this generation has no hope for what's ahead... I've learned that we used less of our hearts and more of the anger that's in our head... I see that's it's better to cope with hearing our young ones getting shot in the head by creating more broken souls in the devil's bed.

But it's time to open your eyes.

You can't honestly say you're mad at this generation if they were never led...getting up everyday, walking to work on the concrete where our blood had shed.......how has this not moved you yet?

Our children are playing with chalk to outline where they bodies will lay... there are more guns being raised and less knees on the ground to pray...darkness is not scary anymore because the devil have shown himself in the day...What part of this sounds OK?

Open your eyes.

Putting our hands in our pockets are no longer safe. Meeting a cop is a form of our hand raised instead of a handshake... screaming out for help is another sign of keeping your doors lock and letting loud music play... it's not just blacks that is afraid. Its every person who feels like they can't escape.

So how about you open your damn eyes!

See I also used to wait...just sitting there waiting for something to change. But nothing did and what I found was myself in a delay. I am changing that from today. I don't understand how you can slip into a T.V. show stage where you know all the episodes and the character's name, yet you turn the other cheek when another body is being slain, I guess that's not the show that's important enough around 8. Let's just stop and do a commercial break....

Ok, commercial over now open your eyes.

I'm getting sleepless.... I'm real tired of us subtracting our souls for temporary satisfaction. Acting as if we don't know what the hell is happening so these sites that are broad cast on FB or IG has become the latest tourist attraction. When are we going to unite and add common sense because it seems that's what our children are lacking.

I'm no Dr. King but I can't hear freedom ring…the only familiar ring is the sirens from the police. The familiar ring is people screaming from the top of their lungs" it's not fair we are minorities". Who the hell told you these things?! We are kings and queens and our throne are having control of the streets so stop with the stupidity and stop accepting these name callings. Don't you see?

Men, Ladies…Please open your eyes.

Monday through Wednesday you complain about life daily, Thursday you slipped into throwback past to run from reality, Friday through Saturday you become a new personality which consists of partying and rachetry and then Sunday is asking god to get you through the week…. You have forgotten your strength and fell in love with weak…. Your mouths may not talk but your tears surely speak...I know these days because you were once me... but it's time to stop claiming your happy and become free.

Let's see...who will open their eyes

What would it take? Another rape? Another fight being taped? More dope being baked? More bodies being slain? More holding in pain? Do our people need to be tamed? Do you want them to put us in a cage? Is it still funny to plank? Not knowing in the ships, slaves were doing the same? What are we to do? Saying we excelled to another level but not ready to face another devil. We are making ourselves look like fools!

Look around you…. Is this peace? Is it? Or is it the feeling of being free for a moment until another tragedy comes to visit.

Can you see? Seriously? And don't say barely because even she was another joke we seem to carry. Rumor has it, it's her body now they buried.

This generation is dying...quickly- that shit doesn't seem scary? ... not knowing that you're just living to die something mothers can relate to Virgin Mary. So, tell me after hearing this.... what are you waiting for.... are you going to make a change...or do the unchanged and shut your windows and close your doors..

When will our eyes be open?

A CONVERSATION WTH YOUR INNERCHILD

SAVE YOURSELF

Repeat after me: "I am important, I love myself more than anyone in this world and I will save myself before saving others"

What does it mean to "Save yourself"?

Save yourself like you save the battery life on your phone. What do I mean by this? What is the percentage on your phone now? High or low: If your phone was dying naturally our instincts tells us to do 2 things: Ask someone if they have a charger or if you have a charger, immediately charge your phone. Something so simple. Why is that? We programmed our mind to think if our phone died then that's a bad thing, so we go into protective mode. We do the same thing with everything outside of us.

In a relationship for instance, most people tend to see that their partner is spiritually, mentally or emotionally dying...losing percentage of life. Naturally because we love them, we want to charge them back to being 100%. So, we find ways to get them back on their feet and at first, it's a great thing because that's what you do in a relationship. But what happens every time you find yourself always charging their battery? They seem to get to a lower percentage faster than before and now has become dependent on your energy and has lost their own energy they had in the first place when you guys first met. Then things start to change. They don't seem to be charged for a long point of time and your outlet starts to feel drained. Yet you continue to put all this energy you have left and now your energy is no longer being shared but it's being sucked in. You become frustrated and emotional and may even turn emotionless because you gave it all away leaving you with nothing left.

Now of course this may happen over a few months, years or sooner than you thought. Either way it happened. Why? We forget to save ourselves. Most empaths internalized energies good and bad while trying to save everyone that need help which is unhealthy. Subconsciously we are inputting toxicity in our bodies every time we exchange bad energy for our good energy. Saving yourself is about tapping into the subconscious mind. Being aware of what we do naturally and monitoring that. Its ok to help people but it's not ok to help people while depriving yourself. Its ok to love people but it's not ok to love people more than yourself. Its ok to be there for people but it's not ok to make yourself second in your **own** life. This is where being selfish is ok because it is impossible to do anyone good if you can't give yourself that 100% first. Most people who tend to have a "Big heart" are more likely to be bait for negativity because they are willing to open themselves up without thinking twice.

It is not taught that thinking twice is a good thing. You must think with your emotions and then you must think with your mind. If they don't agree then it's not the right energy. You must make time for yourself. Love yourself enough to know that time works for you. You don't work for time. Understand that you can't save anyone that's not willing to save themselves first. You also can't do the leg work for a person who doesn't like to run. Even when temptation arise and your tempting to pick up a phone when someone who sucks your energy calls, or answer a text when everyone and their mother is hitting you up or when someone is in need of your energy, make sure you talk to yourself and ask yourself :Do I have enough energy to spread for others at this moment? Have I given myself 100% of me first before I donate some energy" What have I done to make myself feel good, make me feel happy or at peace before I do this for another person" Your sanity and your spirit should always be aligned before donating your time. If you are having an off day and your spirit is not right, its ok to tell someone: "I am sorry but where I am at spiritually, emotionally or mentally at this moment, I am unable to give you my time." You think they might be super upset but 9 out of 10 they will understand because they been there before. Most of our worries of not being there for someone is just in our heads.

EYE SURVIVED

Howard Thurman who is a civil rights leader who dies in the 80" s once said, *"Don't ask yourself what the world needs. Ask yourself what makes you come alive, and go do that, because what the world needs is people who have come alive."*

What good would it be if you're walking dead. Walking with no life, no energy because you allowed leeches to feed on you. We take on bad behavior patterns and not saving yourself is one of the common ones. If you can read people feelings and energies very well and people are drawn to you, or you always end up helping everyone with no hesitation, most likely you are an empath and recognizing that you're an empath is the first step in taking charge of your emotions instead of constantly drowning in them. Staying on top of empathy will improve your self-care and relationships.

You must fall in love with your spirit first before loving or falling in love with someone or something else. This world needs you to save yourself because your spirit and wisdom is greatly needed. Start dating yourself. See what you like and don't like. Allow yourself be kind to yourself. Give yourself compliments, stare at yourself in the mirror, pat yourself on the back, love on yourself as if you're the only person in this world that needs it. Start saying the word "**no**" more often to others and start saying "**yes**" more to yourself. Pay attention to your pattern behavior. Write down the things you allowed in your space that doesn't show that you're saving yourself. Become aware of your energy and actions when someone is requesting your time. Keep a journal and write everything down then start taking it day by day of changing how you respond to others versus how you respond to yourself. You will see a big improvement but and you will feel so good about yourself! This is what saving yourself is about. Learning to have an open slot that's timeless for your soul. To pamper yourself with love and gifts.

*I CHALLENGE YOU: When you are done reading, write down one thing you are going to start doing that surrounds "Saving yourself" and within two weeks and if possible, via email, I want to know an update with how you have been saving yourself?

EYE SURVIVED
EXPRESS YOURSELF!

How did you feel reading this book? Were you able to start your journey to heal with me? I hope so! Once last thing you must do before closing this book! You must release! These few pages are simply for you to release, let go of all the toxic thoughts and energy! You can be creative with markers, colored pencils, stickers or just a pen/pencil expressing yourself freely! You ready? Let's RELEASE!

EYE SURVIVED

EYE SURVIVED

****

Awesome!! You are NOW done with this book this does not mean you are done with Healing! Enjoy the journey! I am so happy and grateful that you took the time to heal with me! To survive with me! Thank you!

"Without Readers, Stories Wouldn't Exist"-

IG: Eye_Survived_

ACKNOWLEDGMENT

First and foremost, I thank God for keeping me throughout all I been through. For showing me the purpose of my living!

To my big sister, Ada Medina who took the mother role at 11 years old and have endure so much just so I can live! Thank you for taking me in and becoming my "Sister Mom" I needed. You loved me the best way that you could have, and I will always be grateful for you! We been through so much together! We are both healing now!

To my older brothers, Alex Escalera and Miguel Medina, I understand now. I understand the tough love you've given me. You didn't want me to go through what you went through and I will always love you! Thank you for surviving with me!

To my spiritual mom, Errica Mitchner! You have saved my inner child from dying in 2011! Thank you for taking me and Carmen in and creating a better life for us in Baltimore, MD! God has showed his love through you! I love you!

To my best friends from childhood, I will always love you guys! The late-night talks, laughter and cries we have become each other warriors!

To my relationships I have had, thank you. We were just crayons trying to create a perfect picture- even when we colored outside the lines. Thank you for loving me! I will always have love for you!

To all of my family in New York, my artists family, Sonia Speaks & HOD, and everyone else who have listened, prayed, supported and became a part of my life, THANK YOU! You are part of my healing and I will forever be grateful for your love!

Saving the best for last, my daughter Carmen Gladys Muriel. You are an angel in human form. Since you were born January 3rd, 2007 my life has changed. Every day you saved me from the evil of this world. You are magical and I am blessed to have you as a daughter! Thank you for being the light this world needs! Mommy loves you so much!

To my parents and son in heaven, I hope I made you proud.

To the reader, thank you! Thank you for healing with me! I pray you share this with your friends and family so they too, know they can get through life as well! I pray you are strong enough to share your OWN story! You are and will always be a **SURVIVOR!**